T0381375

MAMA AND ME

Author: Shelia Harrison

To order additional copies of this book, contact:
Xlibris
844-714-8691
www.Xlibris.com
Orders@Xlibris.com

ISBN: Softcover   978-1-4535-5883-6
        EBook   978-1-6641-4740-9

Print information available on the last page

Rev. date: 12/09/2020

Dedication

A.J. and I would like to say thanks to the city of Arnold for receiving us and helping us in our time of need. Special thanks to the teachers and staff at Fox Elementary. Thank you for all you have done for me and my son. To Dan and Judy Fisher for helping us with food as well as room and board. To Joyce Meyers Ministry for helping with gas, as well as room and board. To my Spiritual Mother Gladys Marrero and her daughter Cheryl Mitchell who lives in California, answered a call from a friend that they have not heard from in years, thank you for your financial support. To Jackie and Carlene Spears who live in Tennessee for helping with food, gas, money, and transportation. Last but not least to one of the best Pastor I know Elder Eddie Whitelaw for helping with food, gas, room, and board. All of these people kept A.J. and me from being homeless in Missouri and sleeping in the van. We are eternally grateful, all the homeless people that are sleeping on the streets of America today, God's hand of Mercy and Favor was upon us. Special thanks to my daughter Ariel Harrison for her sacrifice of love in helping me with transportation, financial support, and with the editing of this book. May God forever smile on you, and we bless you in the name of our Lord and Savior Jesus Christ.

MAMA AND ME

Introduction

    This book is written in honor of my son A.J. who was eleven years old when we started our journey to Missouri. After being married for thirty years I found myself starting over as a single mom. A.J. would always say, "We are going to make it Mama, and we will be happy." We are happy today starting our lives over and are very grateful to our Creator that things are as well as they are. Always find something in your life to be grateful for because there is someone that is not as fortunate as you are. You are special to me in every way A.J., and I love you dearly.

"Good morning A.J. said Mama. I decided that we should move to Missouri to start our life over. How do you feel about moving to Missouri?" A.J. stated, "It is alright with me Mama."

Mama said, "I am not sure where we will live when we get there, we might have to sleep in the van until I find a place. Will you be ok with that?" "Yes, Mama!" A.J. exclaimed.

"I will call your school to request that they have your records ready when I pick you up."

When Mama arrives at the school, she goes into the office, "I am here to get A.J., and do you have his records ready? The receptionist replied "Yes, where are you moving to?" "We are going to Missouri; I am not sure which city but somewhere close to St. Louis." The secretary asked "Do you have any relatives there?" Mama replied "No, but I am trusting in the Creator by faith that this is the right thing to do at this time."

Mama loaded up the van with some clothes, food, microwave, pillows, and plenty of cover. She only had two hundred and seventy-five dollars to get there, she hoped that is enough.

As me and Mama traveled toward Missouri I was excited about going somewhere new.

Mama did not know exactly where in Missouri we would stop until she stop for gas and the attendant told her about Arnold Missouri. Mama said, "That is where we will go A.J.! Arnold here we come."

"Look A.J. there is the exit for Arnold; we will get off on the next exit."

When Mama pulls off to the right and made a left turn, there was Fox Elementary School sitting on the left side of the street.

We got out of the van and went inside. They immediately enrolled me in school and I started that day. I was in school in Tennessee one day and Fox Elementary the next day.

Their school mission statement was to take in homeless children who had no permanent residence within their area. They gave me school supplies, book bags, and free food coupons for me and Mama.

They also told Mama where to go to get help with a place to live.

Mama went to Family Service Office to sign up for government benefits.

After leaving Family Service Office, Mama went to the Salvation Army.

They gave Mama food and a voucher to get us a place to live.

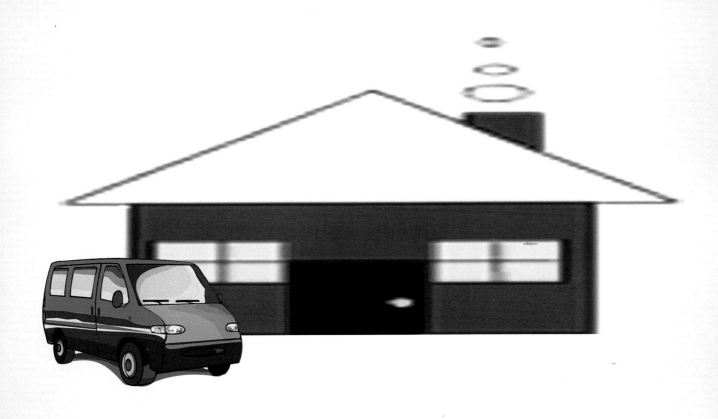

Mama went to the Motel and talked with the manager.

She showed Mama our new home, and Mama said," I will take it."

Mama picked me up from school and said, "A.J. we have a new place to live."

We went back to the motel, and I meet the manager along with her family. They were very friendly and nice.

The manager told Mama, "Never leave A.J. in the motel by himself." Mama told her, I will only look for work during school hours and days until I can find an afterschool program or daycare that I can afford."

When A.J. and Mama got settled, they call their family, friends, and Pastor to let them know that they were safe.

Mama wanted to enroll in Jefferson College where she could continue her education. She was enrolled in Dyersburg State Community College when we left Tennessee.

When Mama and I went to the College she meets an African American woman who invited us to church. We will call her Ms. V, who was very friendly and nice to us.

Ms. V meet us at the service station on the following Sunday in Arnold. The gas station attendant allowed Mama to leave her van in the parking lot while we went to church in St. Louis. Ms. V's church was located in St. Louis, and the members made us feel very welcomed while we visit there.

This was the second church we had visited. The first church was in Arnold where we lived, and I received a scholarship to play basketball. They had the greatest team I had ever seen, it was like a professional league for children.

Mama and Ms. V became best friends, and they still talk on the telephone to this day. We found out that Ms. V was connected to the same church that gave me a basketball scholarship; they were very friendly and nice toward Mama and me.

"You know Arnold is a great place to live and raise a family," Mama told AJ. "I love it here too Mama, and I don't want to go back to Tennessee. Can we stay here?" "If I can find a job, we just may live here a long time."

We never had to sleep in the Van one night. Provision was made for us every day. I guess you can say there were, "Angels looking out for Mama and me."

MAMA AND ME

Author: Shelia Harrison

Printed in the United States
By Bookmasters